THEATRE YEAR

**A selection of photographs by Donald Cooper
of productions in London and Stratford
November 1980 to October 1981.**

With an introduction and index by Michael Coveney.

In (Parenthesis) Limited

For my Mother.

Theatre Year is intended to represent the broad
spectrum of the 200 or so plays which I photograph
each year, out of the 300 to 400 which open
annually in London and Stratford. Apart from the
fact that it is physically impossible to cover
every single production, a selective process has
to apply in order to keep Theatre Year reasonably
compact and visually interesting.

Resounding failures and bizarre oddities may well
be included, especially if they provide a striking
image for the record, but mediocre productions
yielding indifferent photographs are generally
omitted. Some productions which by any criteria
should have been included – for instance *Virginia,
Barnum* and *The Sound of Music* – do not appear
because photographic facilities were not made available.

Despite the inevitable element of subjectivity
involved in the selection process, I hope that
Theatre Year achieves a fair balance and proves
to be a valuable and interesting record of
another year's productions.

The dates listed refer to the official Press nights.
There is also an index which comprises annotated
production details and an alphabetical list of titles.
Every effort has been made to ensure the accuracy of
the information given, and corrections for any
errors made would be gratefully received.

Donald Cooper London October 1981

Front cover:
Elaine Page *Grizabella*; *Cats* New London
Roger Rees *Nicholas*; David Threlfall *Smike*; *Nicholas Nickleby* Aldwych
Dinsdale Landen *Zangler*; *On the Razzle* Lyttelton

Published by In (Parenthesis) Limited
21 Wellington Street, London WC2

Printed in England by Battley Brothers Printers, Clapham, London SW4 0JN
Designed by Michael Morris

Introduction
By Michael Coveney,
drama critic of the Financial Times.

In a year of come-backs and cut-backs the London theatre fretted its way through a miserable summer of dark and half-empty houses and mounting paranoia over what the Arts Council might be proposing around Christmas time. The Old Vic, having suffered *The Relapse*, finally closed on 16 May with a reported deficit of £400,000 despite the arrival by post of a £5 note from an elderly well-wisher and shouts of Arts Council treachery from Timothy West (himself the Judas of 1980 according to the director of O'Toole's *Macbeth*).

The tills were alive with the sound of muzak at the Apollo, Victoria; *Barnum* and Michael Crawford took the Palladium by storm; musical cat-lovers camped out on the pavement in Drury Lane. These were rare signs of enthusiasm. The Society of West End Theatres (SWET) opened a half-price ticket booth in Leicester Square and almost every show in town was chalked up on a board facing the drenched and bewildered faithful.

At last, and slowly, SWET is coming to realise that things will never be the same again. Jessie Matthews and Nigel Patrick died. *Steaming*, a play about ladies baring their souls, bums and boobs in a Turkish bath (a sort of pseudo-intellectual *Pyjama Tops*) moved into the picturesque Comedy Theatre in its (the theatre's) centenary year. Dario Fo, the anarchic Milanese playwright, was given a rip-roaring reprise at the Criterion with *Can't Pay? Won't Pay!*, which advocated the plunder of supermarkets by destitute house-wives on the eve of the Royal Wedding.

While it is true – as it was in the 1930s – that copper-bottomed escapist entertainment might be the answer to the theatre's prayer, it was depressing to find a full-dress, self-regarding First Night audience at *The Mitford Girls* quaffing free champagne in the interval of a tawdry homage to a vanished era. I was reminded of a wonderful song in a David Hare play of a few years back, 'Last Orders on the Titanic'. I had no objection to the show's subject matter or galumphing triviality; just to the laziness of conception, dire score and lack of edge. I was still trying to sort out which sister was which as the curtain fell.

Two key post-War companies – the English Stage Company at the Royal Court and Theatre Workshop at Stratford East – celebrated their 25th anniversaries before wondering if they would still be in business next year. John Osborne bemoaned the march of the troglodytes on Sloane Square, complaining about plays invariably written by 'Les' and directed by 'Ron'. One of the best new plays in the period under review was, in fact, directed by 'Les' – Les Waters – and the irony was that Paul Kember's *Not Quite Jerusalem*, about a young Cambridge student saying goodbye to all that and setting off for an Israeli kibbutz, was impressively redolent of Osborne's early work.

My top three plays of the year, in order of preference, were Brian Friel's *Translations*, Simon Gray's *Quartermaine's Terms* and Peter Nichols's *Passion Play. Not Quite Jerusalem* jostled along-side such excellent new work as Edward Bond's *Restoration*, Ariane Mnouchkine's *Mephisto* (new to England, at least), Mike Weller's *Loose Ends*, Mike Leigh's *Goose-Pimples* and Mark Medoff's *Children of a Lesser God*. Of these, only the Simon Gray, produced by the redoubtable Michael Codron, originated in the private sector. Weller, Friel and Leigh were all well served at the Hampstead Theatre, the last two moving, respectively, to the National and the Garrick.

Goose-Pimples was like Greek tragedy in the suburbs. The improvisational method yielded, in Antony Sher's portrayal of an Arab mistaking a comfy lounge for the rest room in a brothel, one of the performances of the year. The Foreign Office asked to see a script after objections were raised by a few Muslims, but the smoke was without fire and we were left to speculate on the possibility of Mary Whitehouse objecting to Ben Jonson's puritans or of David McNee to Howard Brenton's policemen.

Mike Weller completed a marvellous trilogy of keenly observed plays about the flower power generation coming through the haze to face each other in the real world, while Mark Medoff's children were the deaf seeking not to be patronised by an educational institution. Trevor Eve and Elizabeth Quinn, teacher and pupil, ensured a rattling success for the new Mermaid and a quick West End transfer.

In directing *Restoration*, Edward Bond let himself down badly. But the sheer ambition of the writing and its scene-by-scene complexity placed it well ahead of most of the year's new work. The idea was to re-write Restoration comedy from the stews up. One of the year's abiding memories will be of Simon Callow as the foppish Lord Are taking breakfast, swearing by last year's breeches, killing his wife and enlisting his livery-man to take the blame – all described in a sumptuous arc of overweening, epigram-ridden callousness.

Translations was the first fruit of the Irish touring company, Field Day, formed last year by Brian Friel and Stephen Rea. In some ways, Friel's rehabilitation in London was the year's most spectacular come-back of all. Variously hailed as a modern classic, the best Irish play since O'Casey, a theatrical disquisition on structuralism, and an evocative slice of rural history, *Translations* seemed to have everything. It was set in a Donegal hedge school of the 1830s. The schoolmaster's elder son returns as an interpreter for the Army who are in the district to produce a new map. This world of casual erudition, mythical place names and fierce communal loyalties is threatened by subtle, then explicit, gestures of imperialism. One scene, where an agent of that imperialism, a young English Lieutenant, makes love to a colleen while she responds in Gaelic (neither understanding the other but weaving a consistent comic pattern in *English*) was unforgettable. En route to the Lyttelton, Ian Bannen acquired a seedy majesty as the bibulous master, his speech a remarkable tapestry of Latin tags, maudlin reminiscence, mocking sarcasm and lip-smacking phraseology.

Quartermaine's Terms was the outstanding item on a pitifully feeble Shaftesbury Avenue agenda. In its setting of a tatty English language school for foreigners in Cambridge and its rigidly inexpressive central character, it combined elements of *Butley* and *Otherwise Engaged*. Unseen characters took on three-dimensional life while poor old Quartermaine (Edward Fox beautifully cast as a square peg in a square hole) emerged as fall guy, confidant, catalyst and victim in the Chekhovian glow of the staff room shuffle. The play came across as an inverted, introverted metaphor of the state of England and there were no better performances all year than those of Prunella Scales, James Grout and Robin Bailey. This is surely Gray's best play to date, mordantly and affectionately written, impeccably directed by Harold Pinter and lovingly lit by Leonard Tucker. All on board were kidding themselves that this was 'a flourishing school' while personal disasters amid the lengthening shades took on the desperate humour of a drowning man complaining about his faulty life-jacket.

There was talk of Albert Finney leading *Passion Play* into the West End, but it seems as though Peter Nichols's technically superlative look at menopausal adultery will have to remain an Aldwych memory from mid-January. The device of giving a married couple fully characterised alter egos was brilliantly exploited by Eileen Atkins, Billie Whitelaw, Anton Rodgers and Benjamin Whitrow. She is a choral society coach, he a picture restorer framed by a 27-year itch. Nichols's private view of love in a bold climate was an innovative invasion of Ayckbourn territory, ravishingly directed by Mike Ockrent and flecked with ironic bursts of ecclesiastical music.

If the West End managements are unprepared to support Nichols on this form, what chance or future is there for younger dramatists? A glimmer of hope was offered by the arrival on the scene of a new impresario Robert Fox (younger brother of James and Edward). He was quick off the mark with *Goose-Pimples* and opened his own account with *Anyone for Denis?* in which Private Eye lampoon was a shot in the arm for a farce tradition stretching back through Brian Rix to Vernon Sylvaine and Philip King. The butler at Chequers, 'Woy' Jenkins, with Warrington still a pipe dream in May, was waiting for power to drop into his lap 'like a wipe fwuit'. Angela Thorne was a blood-freezing Margaret Thatcher much admired by the prototype herself. John Wells's uproarious Denis, padding the panelled lounge in search of snifters, tinctures, lotions and snorts, found himself embroiled in a loony espionage plot along with funny foreigners, drunken chums and two Maggie clones in drag.

At the National Theatre, Don Juan made a double come-back. The rarely performed third act of *Man and Superman*, 'Don Juan in Hell', struck me as slightly tedious, but perhaps that was because the production found no way of animating the convoluted discussion and matching it to the supreme light comedy playing of Penelope Wilton and Daniel Massey as the fencing Shavian lovers. In the Cottesloe, Nigel Terry was a saturnine Don à la Molière.

It was a good year for Miss Wilton, whose Beatrice opposite Michael Gambon's inspirationally cumbersome Benedick in *Much Ado* confirmed her status in the front rank. The best Olivier show was *The Shoemakers' Holiday* directed by John Dexter, a riotous London evening with Brenda Bruce outstanding as the Mayor's *arriviste* spouse and some smokey naturalistic ensemble work reminiscent of Dexter's *A Woman Killed With Kindness* in the National's Old Vic days.

The feature of the Lyttelton was Michael Rudman's casting of black actors in *Measure for Measure* and *The Caretaker* (directed by Kenneth Ives). *Measure* exuded a mood of Caribbean carnival through which Norman Beaton's sour and reserved Angelo stalked his prey in a long black cassock. The same actor's Pinter tramp emerged as a close cousin of Athol Fugard's Boesman. Pinter's London rhythms proved highly appropriate to West Indian speech patterns.

Critical reaction to Tom Stoppard's *On The Razzle* was savagely divided and, while admitting that I hardly cracked a smile all evening, there was much to admire in the work of Dinsdale Landen, Felicity Kendal and, especially, Michael Kitchen. The dream-like enchantment of the grocer boys' one-day razzle in Vienna seemed swamped by Peter Wood's ostentatiously heavy-handed production. The piece was an ambitious attempt to overlay the mechanics of broad farce with punning verbal pyrotechnics, but it was a curiously arid experiment.

The best National production was in the Cottesloe: *The Mayor of Zalamea* by Calderon, a masterpiece of the Spanish Golden Age, moved into the Olivier in December. Michael Bryant as the farmer who embodies the play's vision of peasant honour achieved miracles of understatement in a bone-dry, brow-furrowed performance, and Adrian Mitchell's translation of sinewy prose and octosyllabic lyric poetry was his best theatre writing to date. Otherwise the Cottesloe relied on the beseiged figures of Yvonne Bryceland and Patti Love for its best moments. The former, in Dario Fo's and Franca Rame's *One Woman Plays* was imprisoned by men and economics; the latter, in Arnold Wesker's dour and finally disappointing *Caritas*, by her own religious fervour. The last half hour of *Caritas*, with the 14th-century anchoress vainly renouncing her vows in an anguished monologue was Wesker at his best. The rest was a skimpy taste of the Peasants' Revolt with religious dressing.

The National was really resting on its *Amadeus* laurels. The show, revised and re-cast, came trailing clouds of Broadway glory and bolstered the West End. People who had forgotten what House Full signs looked like passed nostalgically along the Haymarket.

The question here is whether, had Shaffer taken his ingenious pot-boiler (John Simon in New York labelled it 'a middlebrow master-piece') to the West End market in the first place, there would have been sufficient courage or resources to stage it even half as well as at the National. Linchpin of the RSC year was, once again, *Nicholas Nickleby*, another show quite beyond the current ambition and nerve of the commercial sector.

Trevor Nunn spent half his year directing *Cats*, a magnificent sleight-of-hand affair by Andrew Lloyd Webber and the first genuine British contribution to popular dance drama; and setting up the Broadway triumph of *Nickleby*. Still, the RSC intimated that the ground was shifting. A violent challenge to the Nunn/Barton careful ensemble tradition was thrown down by Terry Hands's *Troilus and Cressida*, the first RSC Shakespeare to open in London for years. Together with the import of Hands's 1980 Stratford *As You Like it, Troilus* suggested that the RSC could at last cope with Teutonic excess and remain true to itself. The staging in both cases was breathtaking. Different again was Michael Bogdanov's version of *The Knight of the Burning Pestle*, an inspired, punkish stop-gap on the *Nickleby* set. Contrary to the majority opinion, I felt that everything in *Pestle* made good, accessible sense; a strong cast was superbly led by Timothy Spall and Margaret Courtenay.

Alan Howard adjusted to the RSC small-scale with two of his most brilliant portrayals, in Ostrovsky's *The Forest* and in C. P. Taylor's beautifully directed (by Howard Davies) new play about a well-meaning Nazi sucked into the holocaust, *Good*.

On the main stage in Stratford, the RSC mounted appalling revivals of *The Winter's Tale* and, in John Barton's disastrous double bill, of *Titus Andronicus* and *Two Gentlemen of Verona*. Shallows in the company's acting strength were suddenly revealed. Only Barton's *The Merchant of Venice* and Ron Daniels's inventive, Victorian *A Midsummer Night's Dream* – with the Nunn/Ashcroft *All's Well That Ends Well* still to open in November – salvaged the RSC reputation. Things were not too bright at the box office.

Down the road at The Other Place, however, we had accomplished work from the RSC directorial new guard: Farquhar's *The Twin Rivals* staged with ecstatic fluff and flair by John Caird; *A Doll's House* magnificently done by Adrian Noble with Cheryl Campbell and Stephen Moore hitting the heights; and, by all accounts, a riveting Dekker from Barry Kyle, *The Witch of Edmonton*. The time cannot be far off when Davies, Caird, Noble, Kyle and Daniels start knocking each other out in the competition for ultimate power alongside, or instead of, Nunn and Hands.

Another small rush of new blood was mercifully provided in August by the first London International Festival of Theatre (LIFT), organised by three inexperienced university graduates. The LIFT centre-piece was *Macunaima* from Brazil, a resonant folk tale strained through the influence of Max Ophuls, Fellini and Hal Prince. This showbiz threat to Third World values was precisely the richly ambiguous point of the exercise. A young London audience appeared from nowhere, despite the temporary closure of *Time Out* magazine, and flocked to French performance art, Polish displays of nationalistic *angst*, the brilliant Dutch group Het Werkteater at the ICA with a nifty, touching piece about homosexuality, and even lunchtime solo events from Peru. The festival broke even and another is promised for 1983.

The Mermaid re-opened in the bowels of a Puddle Dock redevelopment scheme on 7 July. Ralph Richardson rang the ship's bell that summoned us to a famous fiasco, a ghastly musical version of the creaky Jacobean comedy *Eastward Ho!*

The Round House, assuming the National's responsibility of bringing regional reps to the capital, offered a temporary home not only to the Glasgow Citizens, but also to the Royal Exchange of Manchester and the Oxford Playhouse. The Oxford *Mephisto* was a stunning piece adapted from a Klaus Mann novel about a group of Hamburg actors between the Wars preserving and compromising their art in the shadow of Hitler. Ian McDiarmid was tremendous as the sold-out star. Manchester provided Adrian Noble's terrific *The Duchess of Malfi* with Helen Mirren, Bob Hoskins and Peter Postlethwaite; a splendid French farce; Max Wall and Trevor Peacock striking a rich vaudevillian vein in *Waiting For Godot*; and Tom Courtenay and Cecilia Richards (the year's best new actress) in a gorgeously costumed *The Misanthrope*.

Out at Greenwich, Alan Strachan kept up the good work with fresh, perceptive revivals of Coward's *Present Laughter* (transferred to the Vaudeville) and Rattigan's *The Deep Blue Sea* in which Dorothy Tutin was at her very best and least-mannered. Maggie Smith, too, returned triumphantly in Edna O'Brien's *Virginia* at the Haymarket. J. P. Donleavy proved once again that he has not yet found a theatrical equivalent for his scintillating novels in a brash, misguided adaptation of his own *The Beastly Beatitudes of Balthazar B*, and Penelope Keith in *Moving* did enough and more to suggest that Stanley Price's play, more thoughtfully written, could have been an astringent, enduring addition to the modern repertoire.

The final throw-back was to the era of New Orleans jazz in *One Mo' Time!* at the Cambridge, but I was too busy jumping up and down on my seat to either notice or care. Among 25 great songs, Sylvia 'Kuumba' Williams's knockdown versions of two Bessie Smith classics were high spots of technical prowess and sexual innuendo. Perhaps, as usual, it wasn't too bad a year after all.

1 John Cowley *O'Higgins*; Brian Hayes *Joe*

The Irish Play The Warehouse 18 11 80

2 Sally Brelsford; Sheila White *Mary Pickford*; Jane Hardy *Wally*

The Biograph Girl Phoenix 19 11 80

3 Leslee Udwin *Gila*; Philip Davis *Mike*

Not Quite Jerusalem Royal Court 2 12 80

4

Don Juan Round House 3 12 80

5 Malcolm Storry *Clive Heap*; Richard O'Callaghan *Roy Boyd*; Ron Cook *Mark Craven*

6 Karl Johnson *Paul Prior*; Ron Cook

Television Times The Warehouse 9 12 80

7 Frederick Warder *Hiawatha*; Terry Diab *Minnehaha*

Hiawatha Olivier 10 12 80

8 Ann Lynn *Olwen Peel*; Anthony Daniels *Gordon Whitehouse*; Stacey Dorning *Betty Whitehouse*; Peter Dennis *Charles Stanton*; Jennifer Daniel *Freda Caplan*; Clive Francis *Robert Caplan*

Dangerous Corner Ambassadors 17 12 80

9 James Saxon *Deirdre*; John Dicks *Pearl*; Lesley Duff *Cinderella*

The Amusing Spectacle of Cinderella and Her Naughty-Naughty Sisters Lyric Hammersmith 17 12 80

10 Olivier Pierre *Felix*; Susan Hampshire *Elisabeth*

The Revolt New End 17 12 80

11 Eileen Atkins *Nell*; Billie Whitelaw *Eleanor*

12 Benjamin Whitrow *James*; Louise Jameson *Kate*;
Anton Rodgers *Jim*

Passion Play Aldwych 13 1 81

13 Lynn Farleigh *Simone*; Jennifer Piercey *Giselle*; Matyelok Gibbs *Mme Laurence*; Sandy Ratcliff *Mimi*; John Levitt *Max*;
Brenda Cavendish *Marie*

The Workshop Hampstead Theatre 14 1 81

14 Trudie Styler *Desna*

Naked Robots The Warehouse 19 1 81

15 Elizabeth Bradley *Mother*; Marjorie Yates *Sandra*; Mike Packer *Johnny*; Jean Boht *Mary*; Anna Keaveney *Bridie*

16 Peter Jeffrey *Frank Gladwin*; Miranda Richardson *Jane Gladwin*; Barbara Ferris *Liz Ford*; Penelope Keith *Sarah Gladwin*

17 Basil Henson *Roebuck Ramsden*; Penelope Wilton *Ann Whitefield*; Barbara Hicks *Miss Ramsden*; Timothy Davies *Octavius Robinson*; Anna Carteret *Violet Robinson*; Daniel Massey *John Tanner*

18 Peter Welch *Irishman*; Greg Hicks *Hector Malone*; Penelope Wilton; Timothy Davies; Anna Carteret; Basil Henson; Daniel Massey

Man and Superman Olivier 22 1 81

19 Daniel Massey *John Tanner*

20 Daniel Massey; Penelope Wilton
Ann Whitefield

21 Michael Bryant *the Devil*; Penelope Wilton *Doña Ana*; Basil Henson *the Statue*

Man and Superman Olivier 22 1 81

22 Maureen O'Brien *Amanda*; Simon Butteriss; Celia Fox *Berinthia*

23 Henry Moxon *Bull*; John Nettles *Lord Foppington*

The Relapse Old Vic 27 1 81

24 Lesley-Anne Down *Eliza Doolittle*   25 Lynda Bellingham   26 Lorraine Chase

Pygmalion Young Vic 28 1 81 6 3 81 18 8 81

27 Gwen Watford *Monica Reed*; Donald Sinden *Garry Essendine*; Dinah Sheridan *Liz Essendine*

Present Laughter Greenwich 29 1 81

28 Ronald Pickup *William Mossop*; Stephen Reynolds *Fred Beenstock*; Roger Alborough *Albert Prosser*;
Arthur Lowe *Henry Horatio Hobson*; Julia McKenzie *Maggie Hobson*; Lesley Manville *Alice Hobson*;
Veronica Sowerby *Vickey Hobson*

29 Julia McKenzie; Ronald Pickup

Hobson's Choice Lyric Hammersmith 2 2 81

30 Roger Rees *Semyon*; Emily Richard *Cleopatra*; Susan Tracy *Maria*; Lila Kaye *Serafima*

The Suicide Aldwych 4 2 81

31 Robin Herford *Matthew*; Lavinia Bertram *Caroline*; Graeme Eton *Ivor*; Tessa Peake-Jones *Joanna*; Russell Dixon *Naylor*; Marcia Warren *Jilly*

32 Jack Shepherd *James Dalton*; Michael Elphick *Hawkshaw*   33 Paul Copley *Robert Brierly*; Rebecca Saire *May Edwards*

The Ticket-of-Leave Man Cottesloe 12 2 81

34 Bill Flynn *Pozzo*; John Kani *Vladimir*; Peter Piccolo *Lucky*; Winston Ntshona *Estragon*

35 Francesca Annis *Natalya Petrovna*; Nigel Terry *Mikhailo Alexandrovich Rakitin*

36 Caroline Langrishe *Vera Alexandrovna*;
Francesca Annis

A Month in the Country Olivier 19 2 81

37 Rowan Atkinson

Rowan Atkinson in Revue Globe 19 2 81

38 *the Angelettes*

39 Henderson Forsythe *Sheriff Ed Earl Dodd*;
Carlin Glynn *Mona Stangley*

The Best Little Whorehouse in Texas Theatre Royal, Drury Lane 26 2 81

40 Stephen Lewis *Teddy*   41 Patrick Magee *Frank*   42 Helen Mirren *Grace*

Faith Healer Royal Court 2 3 81

43 Jill Baker *Frankie*; Antony Sher *Muhammad*; Marion Bailey *Jackie*

44 Jim Broadbent *Vernon*; Jill Baker

45 Antony Sher

46 Paul Jesson *Irving*; Marion Bailey

Goose-Pimples Hampstead Theatre 3 3 81

47 Oliver Ford Davies *Eadweard Muybridge*

Snap New End 5 3 81

48 Constance Cummings *Isabel Hastings Hoyt*; Angela Thorne *Virginia*

The Golden Age Greenwich 12 3 81

49 Barbara Windsor *Kath*; Dave King *Ed*

Entertaining Mr Sloane Lyric Hammersmith 18 3 81

50 Diane Langton *Heather*; Ben Cross *Joe*

I'm Getting My Act Together and Taking It on the Road Apollo 31 3 81

51 Helen Mirren *The Duchess of Malfi*; Bob Hoskins *Daniel de Bosola*

52 Mike Gwilym *Ferdinand*; Helen Mirren

The Duchess of Malfi Round House 1 4 81

53 *Fire in Point St Charles*

Balconville Old Vic 2 4 81

54 Charlotte Cornwell *Sarah*; Kate Williams *Rita*; Sandy Ratcliff *Maggie*; Michael Elphick *Sniffer*; Marc Sinden *Charles*;
   Helen Gemmell *Kathy*; Henrieta Baynes *Julie*; Lesley Manville *Lizzie*; Anita Dobson *Vera*

Chorus Girls Theatre Royal, Stratford E15 6 4 81

55 Nigel Terry *Don Juan*; Ron Pember *Sganarelle*

Don Juan Cottesloe 7 4 81

56 T. P. McKenna *Dr Hickey*; Anna Massey *Isobel Desmond*; Stuart Burge *Peter*; Tony Rohr *James*; Veronica Duffy *Mary*;
Harriet Walter *Lily*

57 Harriet Walter; Alan Rickman *Mr Aston*

The Seagull Royal Court 8 4 81

58 Peter Chelsom *Ralph*; Andrew Jarvis *Arthur*

The Accrington Pals The Warehouse 10 4 81

59

Measure for Measure Lyttelton 14 4 81

60 Teddy Kempner *George*; Andrew Hawkins *Client*; Sally Nesbitt *Masseuse*; Timothy Spall *Rafe*; Nick Brimble *Tim*

61 Margaret Courtenay *Nell*; Timothy Kightley *George*; Frank Brennan *Policeman*; Neville Jason *House Manager*

The Knight of the Burning Pestle Aldwych 16 4 81

62 Timothy Kightley; Margaret Courtenay; Teddy Kempner; Timothy Spall *Rafe, and his followers*

63 Timothy Spall *Rafe*

64 Clive Arrindell *Jasper Merrythought*;
Lucy Gutteridge *Luce Venturewell*

The Knight of the Burning Pestle Aldwych 16 4 81

65 Robert Powell *Marlowe*; Pauline Moran *Miss Wanderly*

Private Dick Lyric Hammersmith Studio 21 4 81

66 Tom Wilkinson *Antonio*; Sinead Cusack *Portia*; David Suchet *Shylock*; Brett Usher *The Duke of Venice*

67 Rob Edwards *Launcelot Gobbo*; Jimmy Gardner *Old Gobbo*

68 Sinead Cusack; Jonathan Hyde *Bassanio*

69 Judy Buxton *Jessica*; David Suchet

The Merchant of Venice Stratford 21 4 81

70 *The Company*

71 *The Vincent Crummles Theatre Company in 'Romeo and Juliet'*

72 *The wall of houses*

Nicholas Nickleby Aldwych 23 4 81

73 Teddy Kempner *Master Percy Crummles*; Lila Kaye *Mrs Crummles*; Rose Hill *Mrs Grudden*; Roger Rees *Nicholas Nickleby*; Christopher Benjamin *Mr Vincent Crummles*; Suzanne Bertish *Miss Snevellicci*; David Threlfall *Smike*; Janet Dale *Miss Belvawney*

74 Roger Rees; Edward Petherbridge *Newman Noggs*

75 Clyde Pollitt *Brooker*; Edward Petherbridge; Griffith Jones *Tim Linkinwater*; John Woodvine *Ralph Nickleby*; Hubert Rees *Ned Cheeryble*

76 Roger Rees *Nicholas Nickleby*; David Threlfall *Smike*

Nicholas Nickleby Aldwych 23 4 81

77 David Bamber *Del*; Tony Guilfoyle *Bob*

78 Carl Chase *Hank Williams*

Hank Williams – The Show He Never Gave Kings Head 28 4 81

79 Susan Hampshire *Stella Drury*; Gerald Harper *Robert Drury*

House Guest Savoy 29 4 81

81 Barbara Leigh-Hunt *Raissa Pavlovna*; Eve Pearce *Oolita*; Paul Whitworth *Bulanov*; Alan Howard; Hugh Ross *Milonov*; Raymond Westwell *Bodayev*

80 Richard Pasco *Shastleevsev*;
    Alan Howard *Nyeschastleevsev*

82 Janine Duvitski *Aksiusha*; Barbara Leigh-Hunt

The Forest The Other Place 29 4 81

83 Jimmy Logan *Jock*; Sylvester McCoy *Stan*

Gone With Hardy Tricycle 30 4 81

84 Simon Callow *Verlaine*; Hilton McRae *Rimbaud*

85 Lynsey Baxter *Mathilde*; Simon Callow

Total Eclipse Lyric Hammersmith 5 5 81

86

Satyricon Phoenix 5 5 81

87 Angela Thorne *Maggie*; John Wells *Denis*

Anyone for Denis? Whitehall 7 5 81

88 Deborah Kerr *Iris Caulker*; Ian Carmichael *Chris Caulker*

Overheard Theatre Royal Haymarket 7 5 81

89

90 Elaine Page
Grizabella

91 Brian Blessed *Deuteronomy*;
Wayne Sleep *Quaxo*

92 Finola Hughes *Victoria*; Paul Nicholas *Rum Tum Tugger*

Cats New London 11 5 81

93 Ron Flanagan *Doalty*; Anna Keaveney *Bridget*; Ian Bannen *Hugh*;
   Máire ni Ghráinne *Sarah*

Translations   Hampstead Theatre 12 5 81

94 Brian Cox *Vicomte Robert de Trivelin*; Susan Littler *Zézé*

95 Colette O'Neill *Gertrude*; Frank Grimes *Hamlet*

Hamlet Theatre Royal, Stratford E15 20 5 81

96 Norman Beaton *Davies*; Troy Foster *Mick*; Oscar James *Aston*

The Caretaker Lyttelton 22 5 81

97 Alan MacNaughtan *Burrus*; Siobhan McKenna *Agrippina*; Jonathan Kent *Nero*; Donald Pickering *Narcissus*

Britannicus Lyric Hammersmith Studio 25 5 81

98 John Thaw *Serjeant Musgrave*; Ewan Stewart *Private Sparky*; Patrick Drury *Private Hurst*

99 John Thaw

100 John Thaw; Mary Macleod *Mrs Hitchcock*; Peter Sproule *Private Attercliffe*

Serjeant Musgrave's Dance Cottesloe 27 5 81

101 Eric Peterson *Billy Bishop*

Billy Bishop Goes To War Comedy 3 6 81

102 Philip Donaghy *Lenny Anderson*; Julie Walters *Doreen Thomas*

Having A Ball! Lyric Hammersmith 8 6 81

103 Trevor Peacock *Estragon*; Max Wall *Vladimir*

Waiting for Godot Round House 9 6 81

104 Jane Bertish *Ilona*; Paul Freeman *Bela*

105 Paul Freeman; Allan Corduner *Grigor*

No End Of Blame Royal Court 10 6 81

106 Joseph Chaikin

Texts Riverside 17 6 81

107 Bill Paterson *Josef*

108

109 Alfred Lynch *Simon Eyre*; Brenda Bruce *Margery*

The Shoemakers' Holiday Olivier 19 6 81

110 Natasha Morgan

Room Theatre Upstairs 24 6 81

111 *'Waking Up'* Yvonne Bryceland

112 *'The Same Old Story'*

113 *'A Woman Alone'*

One Woman Plays Cottesloe 26 6 81

114 Miriam Karlin *Mrs Mandrake*; Mike Gwilym *Benjamin Wouldbe*

115 Miles Anderson *Hermes Wouldbe*;
Mike Gwilym ,

116 Harriet Walter *Constance*; Jane Carr *Aurelia*

The Twin Rivals The Other Place 29 6 81

117 Patrick Stewart *Leontes*; Sheila Hancock *Paulina*

118 Leonie Mellinger *Perdita*; Peter Land; John Rogan

119 Gerard Murphy *Young Shepherd*; Geoffrey Hutchings *Autolycus*

The Winter's Tale Stratford 30 6 81

120 Cecilia Richards *Célimène*; Tom Courtenay *Alceste*

The Misanthrope Round House 1 7 81

121 John Harding *Joseph II*; Brian Kent *Johann Kilian von Strack*; Richard O'Callaghan *Wolfgang Amadeus Mozart*; Willoughby Goddard *Count Orsini Rosenberg*

122 Richard O'Callaghan; Morag Hood *Constanze Weber*

123 Frank Finlay *Antonio Salieri*; Richard O'Callaghan

Amadeus Her Majesty's 2 7 81

124 Morag Hood *Constanze Weber*

125 Frank Finlay *Antonio Salieri*

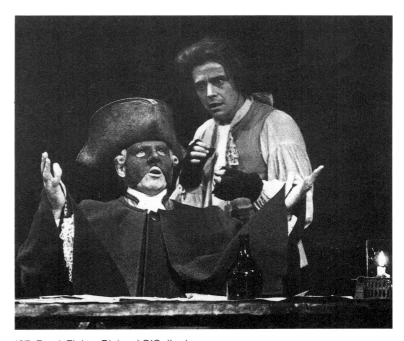

126 Richard O'Callaghan *Wolfgang Amadeus Mozart*

127 Frank Finlay; Richard O'Callaghan

Amadeus Her Majesty's 2 7 81

128 Michael Pennington *Jack Beaty*

129 David Waller *Bill Dunn*

Thirteenth Night The Warehouse 2 7 81

131 Joe Melia *Thersites*

130 Carol Royle *Cressida*; Tony Church *Pandarus*;
James Hazeldine *Troilus*

132 Chris Hunter *Patroclus*; David Suchet *Achilles*

Troilus and Cressida Aldwych 6 7 81

133 Georgina Hale *Josie*; Ann Lynn *Nancy*; Brenda Blethyn *Dawn*; Patti Love *Jane*; Maria Charles *Mrs Meadow*; Jo Warne *Violet*

Steaming Theatre Royal, Stratford E15 6 7 81

134 Philip Sayer *Sir Petronel Flash*; Vivienne Ross *Mistress Touchstone*; Anita Dobson *Gertrude*; Richard O'Brien *Quicksilver*

Eastward Ho! Mermaid 7 7 81

135 Marjorie Bland *Mrs Linde*; Cheryl Campbell *Nora*

137 Cheryl Campbell; Bernard Lloyd *Krogstad*

136 Stephen Moore *Torvald*; Cheryl Campbell

138 John Franklyn-Robbins *Dr Rank*; Cheryl Campbell

A Doll's House The Other Place 9 7 81

139 Sylvia 'Kuumba' Williams *Bertha*; Topsy Chapman *Thelma*; Thais Clark *Ma Reed*; Vernel Bagneris *Papa Du*

One Mo' Time! Cambridge 14 7 81

140 Ron Cook *The Historical Event*; Robert Lindsay *Reporter*

How I Got That Story Hampstead Theatre 14 7 81

141 Juliet Stevenson *Titania*; Mike Gwilym *Oberon*

142 Joseph Marcell *Puck*

A Midsummer Night's Dream Stratford 15 7 81

143 Wolfe Morris *Mr Hardache*; Simon Callow *Lord Are*; Philip Davis *Bob*

Restoration Royal Court 21 7 81

144 Steven Berkoff *Steve*; Linda Marlowe *Helen*

Decadence Theatre at New End 21 7 81

145 Maggie Steed *Antonia*; Christopher Ryan *Luigi*; Alfred Molina *Giovanni*; Sylvester McCoy *Grandfather*

Can't Pay? Won't Pay! Criterion 23 7 81

146 David Essex *Lord Byron*; Sara Kestelman *Augusta Ada*

147 David Essex; Simon Gipps-Kent *Boy*

Childe Byron Young Vic 23 7 81

148 Edward Fox *Sir John Quartermaine*; Prunella Scales *Melanie Garth*

149 James Grout *Henry Windscape*; Robin Bailey *Eddie Loomis*

Quartermaine's Terms Queen's 30 7 81

150

Macunaima Lyric Hammersmith 5 8 81

151 Michael Bryant *Pedro Crespo*; Daniel Massey *Captain don Alvaro de Ataide*; Nicholas Selby *Philip II*

The Mayor of Zalamea Cottesloe 12 8 81

152 Penelope Wilton *Beatrice*

153 Michael Gambon *Benedick*; Tim Woodward *Claudio*; Robert Swann *Don Pedro*; Frederick Treves *Leonato*

154 Frederick Treves; Michael Gambon; Caroline Langrishe *Hero*; Tim Woodward; Penelope Wilton

Much Ado About Nothing Olivier 14 8 81

155 Gary Waldhorn *George Schneider*; Maureen Lipman *Jennie Malone*

Chapter Two Lyric Hammersmith 24 8 81

156 Ed Kelly *Orin Dennis*; Trevor Eve *James Leeds*; Elizabeth Quinn *Sarah Norman*

Children Of A Lesser God Mermaid 25 8 81

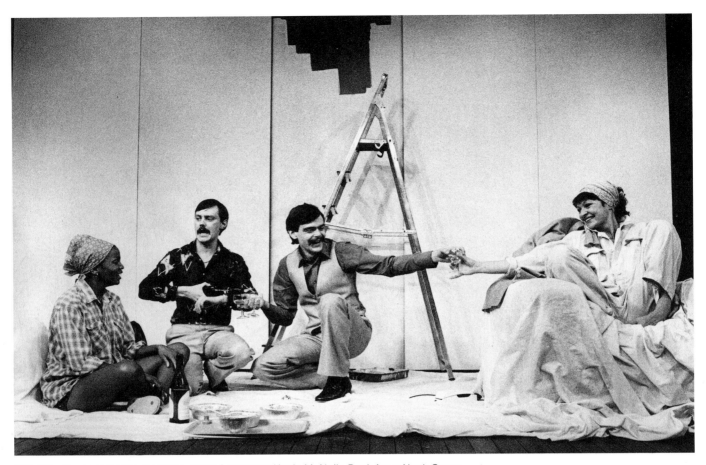

157 Alibe Parsons *Selina*; Ronnie Letham *Lawrence*; Kevin McNally *Paul*; Anna Nygh *Susan*

Loose Ends Hampstead Theatre 26 8 81

158 Margaret Tyzack *Martha*; Paul Eddington *George*

161 David Schofield *Nick*; Mary Maddox *Honey*

159 Margaret Tyzack;
     David Schofield;
     Paul Eddington;
     Mary Maddox

160 Paul Eddington; Margaret Tyzack

Who's Afraid of Virginia Woolf? Lyttelton 27 8 81

162 Sheila Hancock *Tamora*; Bernard Lloyd *Saturninus*

163 Roger Allam *Demetrius*; Leonie Mellinger *Lavinia*; Colin Tarrant *Chiron*

164 Patrick Stewart *Titus Andronicus*; Sheila Hancock; Ray Jewers *Marcus*

Titus Andronicus Stratford 3 9 81

165 Joseph Marcell *Speed*; Geoffrey Hutchings *Launce*; Heidi *Crab*

166 Peter Land *Proteus*; Peter Chelsom *Valentine*

167 Julia Swift *Julia*; Diana Berriman *Lucetta*

168 Leonie Mellinger *Ursula*; Diana Hardcastle *Silvia*

The Two Gentlemen of Verona Stratford 3 9 81

169

170 Rob Edwards *Boris Khomich*;
Dearbhla Molloy *Lyuba
Negnevitskaya*; James Hazeldine
Rodion Nemov

171 Tom Wilkinson *Pavel Gei*; Janine Duvitski *Granya Zybina*; Sion Tudor-Owen *Fiksaty*;
Jonathan Tafler *Zhorik*

The Love-Girl And The Innocent Aldwych 8 9 81

172 Penelope Beaumont *Nurse*; Pip Miller *Freddie*; Felicity Dean *Anne*; Nigel Hess; Nicholas Woodeson *Bouller*; Alan Howard *Halder*; Timothy Walker *Doctor*; Barbara Kinghorn *Mother*; Victor Slaymark

173 Alan Howard; Domini Blythe *Helen*

174 Joe Melia *Maurice*; Alan Howard

Good The Warehouse 9 9 81

175 Jimmy Chisholm *James Boswell*; Nick Ellsworth *Lady Northumberland*

176 Jonathan Adams *Dr Johnson*

Heaven and Hell Royal Court 10 9 81

177 Miles Anderson *Dog*; Miriam Karlin
Elizabeth Sawyer

178 Miriam Karlin; John Rogan *Justice*

179 Gerard Murphy *Frank Thorney*; Juliet Stevenson
Susan Carter

180 Gerard Murphy; Harriet Walter *Winnifrede*

The Witch of Edmonton The Other Place 16 9 81

181 Dinsdale Landen *Zangler*; Michael Kitchen *Melchior*   182 Dinsdale Landen; Felicity Kendal *Christopher*

183 Michael Kitchen; Deborah Norton *Frau Fischer*; Ray Brooks *Weinberl*; Felicity Kendal; Rosemary McHale *Madame Knorr*

On the Razzle Lyttelton 22 9 81

184 Felicity Kendal *Christopher*; Ray Brooks *Weinberl*

On the Razzle Lyttelton 22 9 81

185 Dorothy Tutin *Hester Collyer*; Clive Francis *Freddie Page*

The Deep Blue Sea Greenwich 28 9 81

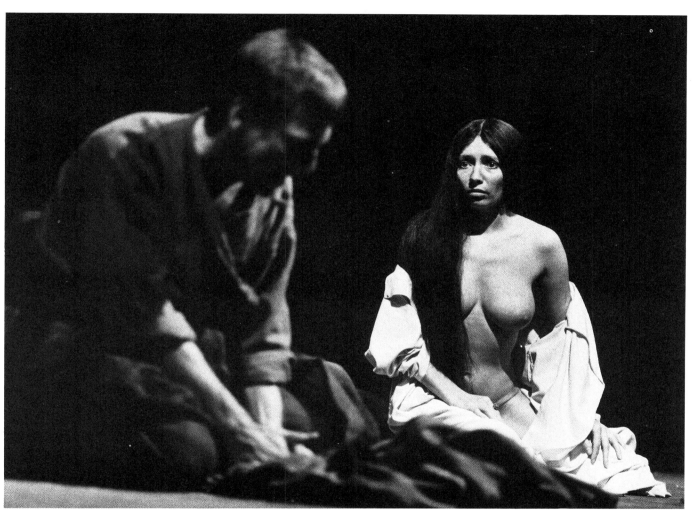

186 Kenneth Cranham *Dorje*; Sharon Duce *Genyen*

Tibetan Inroads Royal Court 29 9 81

187 Patrick Ryecart *Balthazar*; Elizabeth Romilly *Breda*;Charlotte West-Oram *Rebecca*; Simon Callow *Beefy*

The Beastly Beatitudes of Balthazar B Duke of York's 30 9 81

188 Ian McDiarmid *Hendrick Höfgen*; Laura Davenport
Nicoletta von Niebuhr

Mephisto Round House 1 10 81

189 Patti Love *Christine Carpenter*

Caritas Cottesloe 7 10 81

190 Patricia Michael *Diana*; Colette Gleeson *Unity*; Lucy Fenwick *Jessica*; Oz Clarke; Patricia Hodge *Nancy/Muv*; Julia Sutton *Pamela*;
Gay Soper *Deborah*

The Mitford Girls Globe 8 10 81

191 Norman Beaton *Orrin Harris*; Stefan Kalipha *Trevor*; Marty Cruickshank *Kate*

In The Mood Hampstead Theatre 12 10 81

192 Morgan Sheppard *Caesar*; Timothy Dalton *Antony*

193 Carmen Du Sautoy *Cleopatra*;
Timothy Dalton *Antony*

Shakespeare's Rome Mermaid 13 10 81

194 Gwen Taylor *Christine Fenton*; Lynn Farleigh *Marian Wade*; Donald Gee *Ted Fenton*; David Horovitch *Peter Halpern*; Mary Chester *Elizabeth Fenton*; Sylvestra Le Touzel *Juliet*

Harvest Ambassadors 14 10 81

195 Roy Dotrice *Abraham Lincoln*
Mr Lincoln Fortune 22 4 81

196 Richard Huggett *Evelyn Waugh*
A Talent to Abuse Arts 3 8 81

197 Frank Barrie *William Charles Macready*
Macready! Arts 10 9 81

198 Quentin Crisp
An Evening with Quentin Crisp
Mayfair 14 5 81

199 Jeremy Nicholas
Three Men in a Boat Mayfair 15 9 81

Index 1
Production notes
Compiled by Michael Coveney

1 **The Irish Play** by Ron Hutchinson. Presented by the RSC, directed by Barry Kyle, designed by Bob Crowley.

2 **The Biograph Girl** by Warner Brown (book and lyrics) and David Heneker (music and lyrics). Presented by Harold Fielding, directed by Victor Spinetti, designed by John Pascoe, musical staging by Irving Davies, musical direction by Michael Reed.

3 **Not Quite Jerusalem** by Paul Kember. Presented by the English Stage Company, directed by Les Waters, designed by Peter Hartwell. Winner of New Standard Most Promising Playwright Award.

4 **Don Juan** by Robert David MacDonald. Directed and designed by Philip Prowse. Glasgow Citizens' transfer.

5/6 **Television Times** by Peter Prince. Presented by the RSC, directed by Stephen Frears, designed by Mary Moore. First stage play by prominent TV writer.

7 **Hiawatha** adapted from Longfellow by Michael Bogdanov. Presented by the NT, directed by Michael Bogdanov, designed by Marty Flood. Christmas hit for children.

8 **Dangerous Corner** by J. B. Priestley. Presented by Peter Bridge, directed by Robert Gillespie, designed by Robin Archer.

9 **The Amusing Spectacle of Cinderella and Her Naughty-Naughty Sisters** by Martin Duncan. Directed by Martin Duncan, designed by Ultz, choreography by Alain Dehay. Camp, delightfully costumed seasonal extravaganza first seen at Stratford East in 1977.

10 **The Revolt** by Villiers de L'Isle-Adam. 1870 two-hander directed and designed (in collaboration with Liz da Costa) by Simone Benmussa.

11/12 **Passion Play** by Peter Nichols. Presented by the RSC, directed by Mike Ockrent, designed by Patrick Robertson, costumes by Poppy Mitchell.

13 **The Workshop** by Jean-Claude Grumberg, translated by Tom Kempinski. Directed by Nicolas Kent, designed by Stephanie Howard. Oxford Playhouse transfer.

14 **Naked Robots** by Jonathan Gems. Presented by the RSC, directed by John Caird, designed by Ultz, music by Nick Bicât. Punkish lifestyles amusingly threatened by conventional emotional problems.

15 **Touched** by Stephen Lowe. Presented by the ESC, directed by William Gaskill, designed by Frank Conway. Beautiful revival of 1977 Nottingham Playhouse commission.

16 **Moving** by Stanley Price. Presented by Toby Rowland, directed by Robert Chetwyn, designed by Alan Tagg.

17-21 **Man and Superman** by George Bernard Shaw. Presented by the NT, directed by Christopher Morahan, designed by Ralph Koltai, costumes by David Walker.

22/23 **The Relapse** by Sir John Vanbrugh. Presented by the Old Vic Company, directed by Michael Simpson, designed by Adrian Vaux.

24-26 **Pygmalion** by George Bernard Shaw. Directed by Denise Coffey, designed by Carl Toms, costumes by Bob Ringwood. Resilient production making free with both Shaw's stage directions and the film script. The casting of Cockney model Lorraine Chase as Eliza created rare suspense. Could she act 'posh'? She could.

27 **Present Laughter** by Noël Coward. Directed by Alan Strachan, designed by Peter Rice. Donald Sinden and his long-suffering entourage transferred smoothly to the Vaudeville Theatre (17 3 81).

28/29 **Hobson's Choice** by Harold Brighouse. Directed by David Giles, designed by Kenneth Mellor, costumes by Mark Negin.

30 **The Suicide** by Nikolai Erdman. Presented by the RSC, directed by Ron Daniels, designed by Kit Surrey. Brilliant rediscovery of 1930s farcical satire. Transfer via The Warehouse from The Other Place, Stratford.

31 **Suburban Strains** by Alan Ayckbourn. Directed by Alan Ayckbourn, designed by John Hallé, musical direction by Paul Todd. Stephen Joseph Theatre, Scarborough, transfer.

32/33 The Ticket-Of-Leave Man by Tom Taylor. Presented by the NT, directed by Piers Haggard, designed by Robin Don. Interesting 1863 melodrama uncertainly handled.

34 Waiting For Godot by Samuel Beckett. Directed and designed by Donald Howarth. Transfer from the Baxter Theatre, University of Cape Town.

35/36 A Month in the Country by Ivan Turgenev. Presented by the NT, directed by Peter Gill, designed by Alison Chitty. Gill's first NT production notable for Francesca Annis's performance and the blending of the play's outer life and inner voices.

37 Rowan Atkinson in Revue. Presented by Michael Codron, directed by Mel Smith, music by Howard Goodall, designed by Christopher Richardson. West End solo début for clown prince in the Oxbridge wake of Jonathan Miller and John Cleese.

38/39 The Best Little Whorehouse in Texas by Larry L. King, Peter Masterson (book) and Carol Hall (music and lyrics). Presented by Bernard Delfont and Richard M. Mills in association with Universal Pictures, directed by Peter Masterson and Tommy Tune, designed by Marjorie Kellogg, costumes by Ann Roth.

40-42 Faith Healer by Brian Friel. Presented by the ESC, directed by Christopher Fettes, designed by Kandis Cook, lighting by Jack Raby.

43-46 Goose-Pimples. Devised and directed by Mike Leigh, designed by Caroline Beaver. Transferred to the Garrick Theatre (29 4 81).

47 Snap by Nigel Gearing. Presented by Foco Novo, directed by Roland Rees, designed by Adrian Vaux, costumes by Sheelagh Killeen. Imaginative biography of a pioneering Victorian photographer.

48 The Golden Age by A. R. Gurney Jnr. Directed by Alan Strachan, designed by Bernard Culshaw.

49 Entertaining Mr Sloane by Joe Orton. Directed by Kenneth Williams, designed by Saul Radomsky.

50 I'm Getting My Act Together And Taking It On The Road by Gretchen Cryer (book and lyrics) and Nancy Ford (music). Presented by Celia Bogan Ltd and Richard Denning, in association with Theatre Projects. Directed and designed by Word Baker.

51/52 The Duchess of Malfi by John Webster. Directed by Adrian Noble, designed by Bob Crowley, lighting by Geoffrey Joyce, music by George Fenton. Royal Exchange Theatre, Manchester, transfer.

53 Balconville by David Fennario. The Centaur Theatre Company of Montreal directed by Guy Sprung, designed by Barbra Matis. The first bilingual Canadian play.

54 Chorus Girls by Barrie Keeffe (book) and Ray Davies (music and lyrics). Directed by Adrian Shergold.

55 Don Juan by Molière, translated by John Fowles. Presented by the NT, directed by Peter Gill, designed by Alison Chitty.

56/57 The Seagull by Anton Chekhov, new version by Thomas Kilroy. Presented by the ESC, directed by Max Stafford-Clark, designed by Gemma Jackson, costumes by Pam Tait. The ESC's 25th anniversary production re-named the characters and placed them on the West Coast of Ireland with parallel problems of tenants and land-owners.

58 The Accrington Pals by Peter Whelan. Presented by the RSC, directed by Bill Alexander, designed by Kit Surrey. The Great War as experienced by the women left behind in Lancashire.

59 Measure For Measure by Shakespeare. Presented by the NT, directed by Michael Rudman, designed by Eileen Diss, costumes by Lindy Hemming.

60-64 The Knight of the Burning Pestle by Francis Beaumont. Presented by the RSC, directed by Michael Bogdanov, designed by Dermot Hayes, costumes by Chris Dyer.

65 Private Dick by Richard Maher and Roger Michell. Directed by Roger Michell, designed by Liz da Costa, music by Ed Welch. Inventive spoof on Raymond Chandler.

66-69 **The Merchant of Venice** by Shakespeare. Presented by the RSC, directed by John Barton, designed by Christopher Morley. Mellow reading with an unpatronisingly conceived Shylock and a Portia who finds her true self in lawyer's disguise. Quickly moved to the Aldwych (16 7 81).

70-76 **Nicholas Nickleby** by Charles Dickens in an adaptation by David Edgar and the RSC. Presented by the RSC, directed by Trevor Nunn and John Caird, designed by John Napier and Dermot Hayes, lighting by David Hersey, music by Stephen Oliver. Third and last London season for novel theatrical triumph before filming for new Channel 4 TV station and Broadway opening (3 10 81).

77 **Outskirts** by Hanif Kureishi. Presented by the RSC, directed by Howard Davies, designed by Jenny Beavan. Through a decade of time switches, two boys of the 1970s grow apart, racism driving its wedge through South London. Winner of George Devine Award.

78 **Hank Williams – The Show He Never Gave** by Maynard Collins. Directed by Ken Campbell and Terry Canning. First seen at the Liverpool Everyman, this speculative cabaret transferred to the Criterion (2 6 81).

79 **House Guest** by Francis Durbridge. Presented by Michael Codron, by arrangement with Hugh Wontner, directed by Val May, designed by Graham Brown.

80-82 **The Forest** by Alexander Ostrovsky, translated by Jeremy Brooks and Kitty Hunter Blair. Presented by the RSC, directed by Adrian Noble, designed by Bob Crowley. Transferred to The Warehouse (17 7 81).

83 **Gone With Hardy** by David Allen. Directed by Kenneth Chubb, designed by Joe Vanek, music by Andrew Dickson. Charmingly bumptious vaudeville oddity about Stan Laurel.

84/85 **Total Eclipse** by Christopher Hampton. Directed by David Hare, designed by Hayden Griffin, costumes by Carol Lawrence, lighting by Rory Dempster, music by Nick Bicât. Exquisite production of 1968 Royal Court piece, one of the best plays of its generation.

86 **Satyricon** devised by Peter Benedict and Peter Collins, based on Petronius.

87 **Anyone For Denis?** by John Wells. Presented by Robert Fox, directed by Dick Clement, designed by Carmen Dillon, costumes by Jessica Gwynne.

88 **Overheard** by Peter Ustinov. Presented by Louise I. Michaels and Duncan C. Weldon in association with Alexander H. Cohen. Directed by Clifford Williams, designed by Alan Tagg.

89-92 **Cats** by Andrew Lloyd Webber, based on T. S. Eliot's Old Possum's Book of Practical Cats. Presented by Cameron Mackintosh and the Really Useful Company Ltd, directed by Trevor Nunn, associate direction and choreography by Gillian Lynne, designed by John Napier, lighting by David Hersey, sound by Abe Jacob.

93 **Translations** by Brian Friel. Presented by arrangement with Field Day Theatre Company. Directed by Donald McWhinnie, designed by Eileen Diss, costumes by Lindy Hemming. Hampstead Theatre production transferred to the NT's Lyttelton (6 8 81).

94 **Have You Anything To Declare?** by Maurice A. Hennequin and P. Veber, adapted and translated by Robert Cogo-Fawcett and Braham Murray. Directed by Braham Murray, designed by Johanna Bryant. Successful in-the-round version of French farce as good as any Feydeau. Royal Exchange, Manchester, transfer.

95 **Hamlet** by Shakespeare. Directed by Lindsay Anderson, designed by Jocelyn Herbert.

96 **The Caretaker** by Harold Pinter. Presented by the NT, directed by Kenneth Ives, designed by Eileen Diss, costumes by Lindy Hemming. New cast for last year's production.

97 **Britannicus** by Jean Racine, translated by John Cairncross. Directed by Christopher Fettes, designed by Kandis Cook.

98-100 **Serjeant Musgrave's Dance** by John Arden. Presented by the NT, directed by John Burgess, designed by Peter Hartwell, costumes by Pamela Howard. Routine revival of 1959 landmark.

101 **Billy Bishop Goes To War** by John Gray in collaboration with Eric Peterson. Presented by City Productions in association with Mike Nichols, Lewis Allen and the Vancouver East Cultural Centre.

102 **Having A Ball!** by Alan Bleasdale. Directed by Alan Dossor, designed by Bob Crowley. New, slick production of Oldham Coliseum commission set in a vasectomy clinic.

103 **Waiting For Godot** by Samuel Beckett. Directed by Braham Murray, designed by Johanna Bryant. Royal Exchange, Manchester, transfer.

104/105 **No End of Blame** by Howard Barker. Presented by the ESC and the Oxford Playhouse Company, directed by Nicolas Kent, designed by Stephanie Howard, cartoons by Gerald Scarfe. Abrasive, episodic tale of a socialist cartoonist falling foul of authority in both East and West. Exceptional performance by Paul Freeman. Oxford Playhouse transfer.

106 **Texts** by Samuel Beckett, adapted by Joseph Chaikin and Steven Kent. Directed and designed by Steven Kent, lighting by Craig Miller.

107 **Ella** by Herbert Achternbusch, translated by Estella Schmidt and Gavin Muir. Directed by Tim Albery, designed by Hildergard Bechtler.

108/109 **The Shoemakers' Holiday** by Thomas Dekker. Presented by the NT, directed by John Dexter, designed by Julia Trevelyan Oman, lighting by Andy Phillips, music by Dominic Muldowney.

110 **Room** by Natasha Morgan. Presented by That's Not It, designed by Jenny Carey, lighting by Rick Fisher. First seen at the still invaluable Oval House fringe venue, this witty and dream-like event, inspired by a Virginia Woolf polemic, was an enchanting and memorable oddity.

111-113 **One Woman Plays** by Dario Fo and Franca Rame, in a version by Olwen Wymark. Presented by the NT, directed by Michael Bogdanov, designed by Sue Jenkinson and John Bury.

114-116 **The Twin Rivals** by George Farquhar. Presented by the RSC, directed by John Caird, designed by Ultz.

117-119 **The Winter's Tale** by Shakespeare. Presented by the RSC, directed by Ronald Eyre, designed by Chris Dyer.

120 **The Misanthrope** by Molière, translated by Richard Wilbur. Directed by Casper Wrede, designed by Malcolm Pride. Royal Exchange, Manchester, transfer.

121-127 **Amadeus** by Peter Shaffer. NT production presented by Stoll Productions Ltd, directed by Peter Hall, designed and lit by John Bury.

128/129 **Thirteenth Night** by Howard Brenton. Presented by the RSC, directed by Barry Kyle, designed by Bob Crowley. Futuristic thriller re-write of Macbeth which warned, in the fate of a left-wing Cabinet minister, of the dangers of revolutionary socialism.

130-132 **Troilus and Cressida** by Shakespeare. Presented by the RSC, directed by Terry Hands, designed by Farrah, music by Nigel Hess.

133 **Steaming** by Nell Dunn. Presented in association with Eddie Kulukundis, directed by Roger Smith, designed by Jenny Tiramani, lighting by Mick Hughes. Transferred to the Comedy (28 8 81).

134 **Eastward Ho!** by Ben Jonson, George Chapman and John Marston, adapted by Nick Bicât, Robert Chetwyn and Howard Schuman. Directed by Robert Chetwyn, lyrics by Howard Schuman, music by Nick Bicât, designed by Kenneth Mellor, costumes by Mark Negin, choreography by Charles Augins.

135-138 **A Doll's House** by Henrik Ibsen, translated by Michael Meyer. Presented by the RSC, directed by Adrian Noble, designed by Kit Surrey.

139 **One Mo' Time!** by Vernel Bagneris (book) and various others (book and lyrics) including Clarence Williams, Bessie Smith, Ma Rainey, Kid Ory. Presented by Paul Gregg and Lionel Becker by arrangement with Art and Burt D'Lugoff and Jerry Wexler and in association with Shari Upbin. Directed by Vernel Bagneris, designed by Edwin Charles Terrel II, costumes by JoAnn Clevenger, musical direction by Lars Edegran and Orange Kellin.

140 **How I Got That Story** by Amlin Gray. Directed by Nancy Diuguid, designed by Paul Dart.

181-184 **On the Razzle** by Tom Stoppard, adapted from Johann Nestroy's *Einen Jux will er sich machen*. Presented by the NT, directed by Peter Wood, designed by Carl Toms, music by Derek Bourgeois, lighting by Robert Bryan.

185 **The Deep Blue Sea** by Terence Rattigan. Directed by Alan Strachan, designed by Peter Rice, lighting by Mick Hughes.

186 **Tibetan Inroads** by Stephen Lowe. Directed by William Gaskill, designed by Roger Bourke, lighting by Jack Raby. Village blacksmith, superbly played by Kenneth Cranham, caught in a pincer movement of Buddhist tradition and ideological progress after committing adultery with the landlord's wife.

187 **The Beastly Beatitudes of Balthazar B** by J. P. Donleavy. Presented by Naim Attallah, directed by Ron Daniels, designed by Liz da Costa, costumes by Sue Formston. Lumpen adaptation by Donleavy of his own novel sporadically enlivened by Simon Callow.

188 **Mephisto** by Ariane Mnouchkine, translated by Barry Russell. Directed by Gordon McDougall, designed by Nadine Baylis, music by Terry Mortimer, lighting by David Colmer. Oxford Playhouse transfer.

189 **Caritas** by Arnold Wesker. Presented by the NT, directed by John Madden, designed by Andrew Jackness, lighting by Rory Dempster, sound by Rob Barnard.

190 **The Mitford Girls** by Caryl Brahms and Ned Sherrin (book and lyrics), and Peter Greenwell (music). Presented by John Gale and Hinks Shimberg. Directed by Patrick Garland, choreography and musical staging by Lindsay Dolan, dances supervised by Anton Dolin, designed by Stephanos Lazaridis, costumes by Robin Fraser Paye, lighting by Bill Bray, musical direction by John Owen Edwards.

191 **In The Mood** by Michael Abbensetts. Directed by Robin Lefèvre, designed by Sue Plummer, costumes by Lindy Hemming.

192/193 **Shakespeare's Rome** adapted by Julius Gellner and Bernard Miles from *Julius Caesar* and *Antony and Cleopatra*. Directed by Bernard Miles and Ron Pember.

194 **Harvest** by Ellen Dryden. Presented by Colin Brough, directed by Alan Dossor, designed by Eileen Diss, costumes by Jessica Gwynne, lighting by Andy Phillips. First seen at the Birmingham Rep last year.

195 **Mister Lincoln** by Herbert Mitgang. Presented by Theatres Consolidated Ltd, directed by Peter Coe.

196 **A Talent to Abuse** by Richard Huggett. Presented by Dominic March, directed by Simon Basehart, designed by Dave Horn. King's Head transfer.

197 **Macready!** by Frank Barrie. Presented by Eddie Kulukundis and David Conville, directed by Donald MacKechnie.

198 **An Evening with Quentin Crisp** devised by Richard Gollner. Presented by Richard Jackson by arrangement with Julian Courtenay. Seen later in the year at the Duke of York's (12 8 81).

199 **Three Men in a Boat** adapted by Jeremy Nicholas and John David from the novel by Jerome K. Jerome. Presented by Rhombus Productions, directed by Anthony Matheson, designed by Kandis Cook.

Index 2
Alphabetical list of productions